The assassination of Dr. Martin Luther King in May, 1968, was an event which shocked the world. In its violent aftermath the fires of racial fury flared again in more than two hundred American cities. Had all that the world's foremost apostle of non-violence stood for been forgotten? People feared so, but not for long. The Christian message of Martin Luther King, priest, brilliant orator, leader of his people, had struck too deep.

The grandson of a slave, Martin Luther King grew up in a world which regarded all blacks as "second class citizens" – with segregation on buses, in schools, cafes, and most public places. Would this ever change? Many thought it would – but only by terror, bloodshed, revolution. King, too, believed in revolution, but of a different kind.

Combining his Christian principles with those of non-violent political action – the peaceful demonstration, the sit-in – Martin Luther King inspired a movement which was to revolutionize black/white relations throughout America. He gave his people something they had never known – hope for the future. And it was because of this future that a widespread black revolt did not follow his death. That is the real tribute to his greatness.

WAYLAND HISTORY MAKERS

# Martin Luther King

Patricia Baker

WAYLAND PUBLISHERS LONDON

# More Wayland History Makers

*Joseph Stalin* David Hayes and F. H. Gregory
*Goering* F. H. Gregory
*Karl Marx* Caroline Seaward
*Picasso* David Sweetman
*Cecil Rhodes* Neil Bates
*Hitler* Matthew Holden
*The Wright Brothers* Russell Ash
*Jomo Kenyatta* Julian Friedmann
*Al Capone* Mary Letts
*Rommel* F. H. Gregory
*Franco* Richard Kisch
*The Krupps* Mary Letts
*The Borgias* David Sweetman
*Bismarck* Richard Kisch
*Cromwell* Amanda Purves
*Mao Tse-tung* Hugh Purcell

*frontispiece:* Dr. Martin Luther King

SBN 85340 338 4
Copyright © 1974 by Wayland (Publishers) Ltd
49 Lansdowne Place, Hove, East Sussex BN3 1HF
2nd impression 1976
3rd impression 1979
Printed by The Garden City Press Limited
Letchworth, Hertfordshire SG6 1JS

# Contents

# List of Illustrations

# 1. "I Have a Dream"

On 28th August, 1963, 250,000 men and women from all over America gathered at the Lincoln Memorial in Washington D.C. They had come to attend the largest demonstration ever held in America in support of Civil Rights for American Negroes. Restless after a long afternoon of speeches, and tired from standing about in the heat, people were beginning to drift away. Then the main speaker of the day was announced. **The crowd fell completely silent.**

A short, rather stocky black man quietly took the stand. In a prepared speech, he described the problems of Negroes in America. Then, putting aside his text, he said: "I say to you today even though we face the difficulties of today and tomorrow, I still have a dream. It is a dream that is deeply rooted in the American dream. I have a dream that one day this nation will rise up and live out the true meaning of its creed: 'We hold these truths to be self-evident, that all men are created equal.'

"I have a dream that one day on the red hills of Georgia the sons of former slaves and the sons of former slave-owners will be able to sit down together at the table of brotherhood. I have a dream that one day even the state of Mississippi will be transformed into an oasis of freedom and justice.

"I have a dream that my four little children one day

*Opposite* **Martin Luther King giving a stirring speech at the demonstration in support of Civil Rights for American Negroes at the Lincoln Memorial.**

9

Over 200,000 people attended the demonstration for Negro Civil Rights on 20th August, 1963, at the Lincoln Memorial.

will live in a nation where they will not be judged by the colour of their skin, but by the content of their character.

"This will be the day when all of God's children will be able to sing with new meaning 'Let Freedom Ring.' So let freedom ring from the prodigious hilltops of New Hampshire, let freedom ring from the mighty mountains of New York. But not only that. Let freedom ring from every hill and molehill of Mississippi, from every mountainside. When we allow freedom to ring from every town and every hamlet, from every state and

every city, we will be able to speed up that day when all God's children, black men and white men, Jews and Gentiles, Protestants and Catholics, will be able to join hands and sing in the words of the old Negro spiritual, 'Free at last! Free at last! Great God Almighty, we are free at last!' "

The speaker was Martin Luther King, Jr. For eight years this remarkable man devoted his life to the movement for Negro rights in America. His methods, and the quality of his leadership captured the imagination of the whole world.

"A shadow of the plantation and of slavery, a Black Puritan paradise, a presence called trouble, and a tradition of hard work, thrift, service, responsibility, and sacrifice: from this soil came Martin Luther King, Jr." *Lerone Bennett. What Manner of Man.*

# 2. Jim Crow

The Negro Civil Rights movement began in the 1950s in the American South. Almost one hundred years earlier, on 1st January, 1863, Abraham Lincoln had issued the Emancipation Proclamation. With this, as civil war raged throughout the country, America's Negroes were freed from slavery. The war, which lasted from 1861 to 1865, had arisen from this very issue. The Northern States opposed the expansion of slavery and refused to allow it in the newly acquired American territories in the West. The agricultural Southern States, more dependent than the North on slaves (for their cotton and tobacco plantations), saw their whole way of life threatened. They were determined that slavery should be permitted in the Western territories. When Abraham Lincoln, who was opposed to slavery, was elected President of the United States, the South decided to secede, or leave, the Union of the United States. Lincoln retaliated by refusing to let the secessionists use the Federal (national) forts, post offices, and other Federal properties in the South. The result was a long and bloody war -- the American Civil War -- from which the North finally emerged victorious. Lincoln's task was then to improve the lives of American Negroes. He hoped to give them the vote, to build good schools for them, and to ensure that they received the same treatment as whites.

*Opposite* **The Negroes spread the news of Abraham Lincoln's Emancipation Proclamation, which freed them from slavery.**

13

Abraham Lincoln, the American President who issued the Emancipation Proclamation which gave the slaves their freedom.

The white Southerners, however, had no intention of extending equality to their former slaves. Their individual State governments based their policies on the view that Negroes were naturally inferior to white men, and should be kept in a subordinate position. But the laws of the Federal Government took precedence over State laws, and in 1866 a Federal law was passed (the Civil Rights Act) which guaranteed the rights of citizens, regardless of race or colour. The following year, the Federal Government imposed military rule on the Southern States, and guaranteed a State electoral system of "one man, one vote."

For a short time Negroes did enjoy equal rights, taking part in the State governments, and holding public office. However, the Federal Government did not provide economic stability for many of the Negroes in the South. Most Negroes after emancipation had to work for their former owners. There were no other jobs available for them, and they had no money to set up on their own, facts which the white employers turned to their own advantage. Negroes who made use of their civil rights, by voting for example, were threatened with dismissal.

Federal power gradually ceased to protect the rights of the Negroes. American literature, both Northern and Southern, became more and more anti-black, subtly reinforcing the idea of white racial superiority. This hardening attitude allowed new State and local laws to be passed in the South. They were known as "Jim Crow" laws, after a Negro character played by Thomas D. Rice, an American musical entertainer of the mid-1800s.

Jim Crow laws segregated blacks from whites in every public place – restaurants, trains, hospitals, trams, even jails and homes for the blind. By 1907 such segregation applied in every State in the South. The

Federal Government supported it on the grounds that "separate but equal" facilities did not deprive Negroes of their rights.

By the close of the nineteenth century, Negroes again had been relegated to an inferior status in American life. Whites, in both the North and the South, kept their distance from Negroes and did not mix with them socially. Negroes had to create their own social institutions and activities, indeed their own world. And the strongest institution in that world was the Negro church.

The church was a source of strength and comfort for most Negroes. By promising that the suffering endured on earth would lead to great rewards in heaven it helped them to cope with their unhappy lives. Negroes had a very personal idea of God and Jesus Christ; they were sure that God loved them, even if white people did not.

With growing legal and social segregation, racial tension heightened. New problems developed as Negroes, no longer able to live off the land because of economic changes, moved to the towns to look for jobs. But the unions did not accept Negro members, which made it virtually impossible for them to find jobs which paid a fair wage. Competition between poor whites and Negroes for scarce housing led to lynchings and white riots directed against whole areas of the Negro community.

Negroes began to lose faith in Government at every level. As one said, "In the degree that the Southern people stand by in silence and see the Negro stripped of his civil and political rights by a band of unscrupulous men, they compromise their own civil and political freedom . . . If by a mere technicality one class of citizens can be deprived of their rights and immunities . . . what is to prevent any other class from sharing the

> "All persons held as slaves within any State, or designated part of the State, the people whereof shall be in rebellion against the United States, shall be then, thenceforward, and forever, free." *Abraham Lincoln. Emancipation Proclamation.*

15

**Members of the Ku Klux Klan, wearing white robes and hoods, at a ritual burning of the cross.**

same fate?"

Was there any longer any point in looking to the white community for help? Negroes began to make

plans of their own to improve their status. Their most prominent leader and most articulate spokesman at this time was W. E. B. Dubois. He was one of the founders of the National Association for the Advancement of Coloured People; this was a group of prominent white and black Americans pledged to work for the abolition of all forced segregation. To achieve their goals they used legal action and personal persuasion.

At the end of the First World War (1914–18), a militant racialist white organization, the Ku Klux Klan, revived and adopted a plan "... to unite native born, white Christians for concerted action in the preservation of American institutions and the supremacy of the white race." The Klan was responsible for much racial bullying and even lynching. Although it was concentrated in the South, it did have some strength in the North.

As Negroes continued to move to the cities, their self-confidence grew. They became defiant, impatient, aware of their political strength. The Urban League was founded to win them more and better jobs, and the acceptance of Negro members by various unions was a measure of its success.

In 1948 President Harry Truman, the most powerful friend the Negroes had had since Lincoln, banned segregation in all branches of the Federal, civil, and military services. By 1953, Washington D.C. was completely desegregated, and there was a spreading feeling among white Americans that the Negro had been grossly mistreated. Very slowly, that feeling was translated into action. But the key word was slowly.

In the South, hardly anything was being done. Southerners seemed more reluctant than ever to change the social order to benefit the Negroes. So keenly did they feel the threat to their own status, that support for segregation in all its forms became almost a cause.

"The educated Negro of today is a failure, not because he meets insuperable difficulties in life, but because he is a Negro. His brain is not fitted for the higher forms of mental effort; his ideals, no matter how laboriously he is trained and sheltered, remain those of a clown."
*H. L. Mencken, a white American writer who lived 1880–1956.*

# 3. Childhood

Martin Luther King, Jr., was born on 15th January, 1929, in Atlanta, Georgia, in the heart of the American South. He grew up with his brothers and sister in a large house in a middle class section of Atlanta. He had a very happy childhood.

His father, Martin Luther King, Sr., was a preacher at the Ebenezer Baptist Church, one of the richest and strongest black churches in the South. The King family was well-known and respected throughout the locality. Reverend King was not only a dedicated preacher, but also a prominent member of the black community and a leader in civic affairs.

The family was also quite well-to-do, unlike most blacks in the South at that time. Martin was born at the beginning of the great American Depression, a time when millions had no jobs and went hungry. But his family was fortunate and his own life was untouched by these circumstances. The Kings always had enough to eat, good clothes to wear, and a comfortable home. Their life was just like that of any American middle class family, except for one thing: they were black and living in a city where there was great racial discrimination.

Martin was six years old when he first learned what this meant. Nearly everyday until then, he had played with some white children who lived nearby. They were his best friends. However, when they were all old enough

*Opposite* **The church was a source of strength and comfort to most Negroes. They believed that God loved them even if the white people didn't.**

to go to school, Martin had to go to the school for black children, and his friends went to the one for whites. When his friends' mother told Martin not to play with her children any more, Martin demanded to know why. The woman made a few excuses which the boy did not understand, then came the real answer: "They're getting too old to play with niggers."

Martin ran home in tears to his mother. Why had this thing happened? What did it mean? Mrs. King now found herself in a situation every black mother must face at some time. She told her son all about the history of the American Negroes, of the centuries of slavery, and the cruelty and shame of segregation. And she ended by saying, "Don't let this thing impress you. Don't let it make you feel you are not as good as white people. You are as good as anyone else and don't you forget it."

From his father, too, Martin learned about the evils of segregation. He was told to fight it, as Reverend King had always done. A member of the National Association for the Advancement of Coloured People (N.A.A.C.P.) he refused to use segregated lifts, and had fought and won some worthy battles, including one to obtain equal pay for Negro teachers.

When Martin was eight years old, he was again made to feel the shame of racial segregation. His father took him out to buy a new pair of shoes. They sat down in the front of the store. A white shop assistant approached them and said, "If you'll take seats in the back of the store, I'll wait on you."

"Nothing wrong with these seats," said Reverend King.

"But I can't wait on you here."

"We'll either buy shoes, sitting right here, or we won't buy any of your shoes at all," replied Martin's father, and with that he took hold of the boy's hand and walked out of the store. As they went out into the street,

Reverend King told Martin, "I don't care how long I have to live with this thing, I'll never accept it. I'll fight it till I die. Nobody can make a slave out of you if you don't think like a slave."

The Reverend Martin Luther King, Sr., in his church in Atlanta, Georgia.

# 4. Student Preacher

In September, 1944, when Martin was fifteen, he passed the entrance examinations for Morehouse College in Atlanta and began studying there. Morehouse is one of the best Negro Colleges in America, and Martin was impressed by the sense of freedom among the teachers and students. He said of his teachers, "They encouraged us in a positive quest for a salvation to racial ills . . . nobody there was afraid."

The President of Morehouse College was Dr. Benjamin Mays, a preacher. He was to have a great influence on Martin, whom he remembered as "a serious, sensitive boy. He had a balance and maturity then that were far beyond his years, and a grasp of life and its problems that exceeded even that."

Martin was a good student, but did not join in many college activities. He was too busy thinking about his future profession. He thought of studying law, but at the same time he was very drawn to the ministry. Just one thing held him back. He did not like the emotionalism of the Negro church that he knew, with its shouting and hand-clapping. At Morehouse, he heard Dr. Mays preach thoughtful sermons about social conditions. Martin believed this was what a minister should do. To him, helping people to solve their daily problems was just as important as helping them to save their souls.

Through Dr. Mays Martin saw that the ministry

*Opposite* **Martin Luther King preaching in his father's church in Atlanta, Georgia.**

23

could be intellectually respectable, and his personal conflict ended. He decided to become a preacher. He was seventeen years old. When Martin told his father of his decision, Reverend King suggested a trial sermon in the small auditorium at the Ebenezer Baptist Church. As the news of young Martin's sermon spread, so many people came to hear it that it was finally held in the large main sanctuary.

Martin had inherited his father's ability to preach, although his style was far more restrained. His sermon was a huge success. Reverend King, proud of his son, went down on his knees that night and thanked God for the boy's decision to enter the ministry. Shortly after this Martin was ordained and became assistant pastor to his father.

Until now Martin had led a rather sheltered life. He had had no personal experience of the problems of poor black people. So he decided to take jobs during his summer vacations that would give him this. He took unskilled jobs – ones that required backbreaking work,

**In the summer of 1945 Martin worked in the tobacco fields of Connecticut.**

like unloading trains and lorries. He got to know his co-workers well, and saw for himself what it was like to work under white bosses, who called the workers "niggers," and subjected them to all kinds of humiliation. He noticed, too, that when Negroes and whites were doing the same work, the Negro was always paid less.

In the summer of 1945 Martin went North to Connecticut, to work in the tobacco fields there. It was a hard and exhausting job, but it gave him a new experience. Connecticut was in the desegregated part of America, and there, for the first time in his life, Martin could eat in any restaurant and sit in any seat in the cinema. After such an experience, he felt more acutely than ever before the shame of segregation in the South.

Going home by train at the end of that summer, he went to have a meal and was made to sit at the back of the dining car. The waiter pulled a curtain down in front of him to separate him from the white section. "I felt as though that curtain had dropped on my selfhood," he said later.

Martin graduated from Morehouse College when he was nineteen. He went from there to Crozer Theological Seminary, near Philadelphia, Pennsylvania, to study for a Bachelor of Divinity degree. Determined to make the most of his education, he maintained top marks for the three years he spent at Crozer. He also went to philosophy lectures at the nearby University of Pennsylvania, and read book after book on this subject "on a serious intellectual quest for a method to eliminate social evil."

He was particularly impressed with the German philosopher, Hegel, and the American theologian Walter Rauschenbusch. Hegel's theory that world leaders were agents who carry out the will of the "world spirit" he found especially interesting. And of Rauschen-

"Let not the twelve million Negroes be ashamed of the fact that they are the grandchildren of slaves. There is no dishonour in being slaves. There is dishonour in being slave-owners. But let us not think of honour or dishonour in connection with the past. Let us realize that the future is with those who would be truthful, pure and loving. For as the old wise men have said, truth ever is, untruth never was. Love alone binds and truth and love accrue only to the truly humble." *Mahatma Gandhi, writing in Crisis Magazine, July, 1929.*

busch's theory of a social gospel, described in his book, *Christianity and Social Crisis*, Martin said, "It left an indelible imprint on my thinking." Rauschenbusch's idea that the church ought to take a leading role in the crusade for socal justice became part of Martin's own philosophy.

It was also at Crozer that Martin first became interested in the teaching of the great Indian philosopher and leader, Mohandas K. Gandhi. One Sunday afternoon he attended a lecture given by the President of Howard University, Mordecai Johnson, who had just come back from India. Johnson spoke of Gandhi's techniques of non-violent protest to British rule in India, and of his campaign to free India by employing peaceful techniques, such as strikes, boycotts and mass marches. Gandhi had urged his followers to return good for evil, to break unjust laws and to pay the penalty willingly for doing so. "Rivers of blood may have to flow before we gain our freedom, but it must be our blood," he had said.

Martin was so excited by what Mordecai Johnson had said that he immediately went out and bought every book about Gandhi that he could find. He read that Gandhi had himself been influenced by a nineteenth-century American philosopher, Henry David Thoreau. The Indian leader had been in a South African prison when he read Thoreau's *Essay on Civil Disobedience*, which puts forward the idea that jail is the only place for good men when social evil threatens the spirit of man. Thoreau believed that men are duty-bound to disobey evil laws. Gandhi combined these ideas with the teaching of Jesus Christ, and formed his philosophy of non-violence to combat British Rule.

The impact of these ideas on Martin's thinking was tremendous. His "intellectual quest" had reached a turning point.

*Opposite* **The Indian philosopher, Gandhi, whose ideas had a great impact on Martin Luther King.**

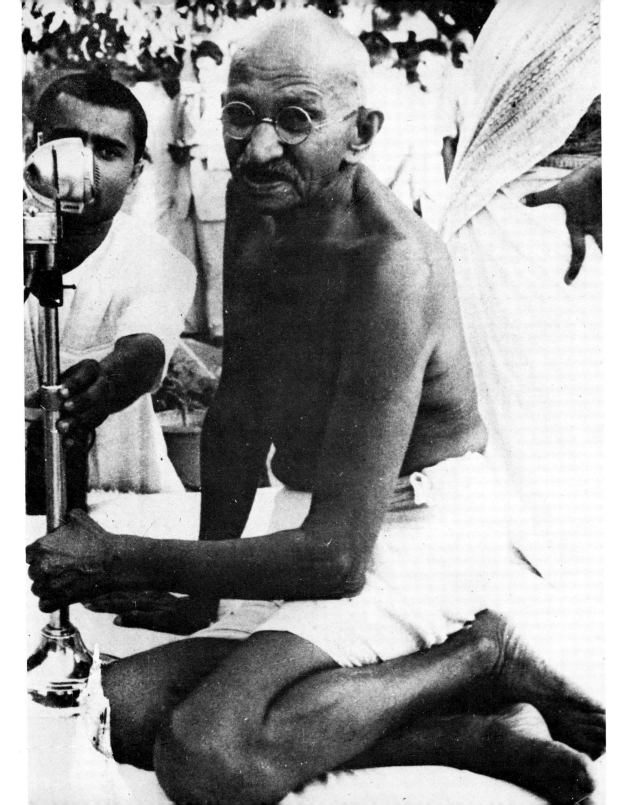

# 5. Coretta

In 1951 Martin Luther King was awarded his Bachelor of Divinity degree from the Crozer Seminary. He left with a brilliant record, "A very bright young man" and, "He seems to know where he wants to go and how to get there," said his professors. He had also won a scholarship of $1,200 to do post-graduate work at the college of his choice. He chose Boston University.

Boston was the home of the philosophy of personalism, a philosophy which emphasized the importance of the individual. King was fascinated by this idea. He believed that "The clue to the meaning of ultimate reality is found in the personality." Later he wrote, "This personal idealism remains today my basic philosophic position. Personalism's insistence that only the personality – finite and infinite – is ultimately real, strengthened me in two convictions; it gave me a metaphysical and philosophical grounding for the idea of a personal God, and it gave me a metaphysical basis for my belief in the dignity and worth of all human personality."

King shared a flat in Boston with an ex-Morehouse classmate and their home became a centre for the black students in the area. He had also started a philosophical club, which held meetings at the flat. A large group of young people, black and white, attended these weekly sessions.

"God called the grandson of a slave on his father's side, and said to him: 'Martin Luther, speak to America about war and peace; about social justice and racial discrimination; about its obligation to the poor; and about nonviolence as a way of perfecting social change in a world of brutality and war.'"
*Dr. Benjamin Mays' Eulogy at Martin Luther King's funeral.*

*Opposite* **Coretta, Martin Luther King's wife.**

29

King had been in Boston only a few months when he met a black student called Coretta Scott, two years older than him. Like him, she had been born in the South, in a small town in Alabama. She had grown up watching her father struggle to make a living for his family on his small piece of land, and had seen him harassed and bullied by white men when he began to make some progress. Once when he had managed to save enough money to buy a saw-mill a white man wanted to buy it from him. He refused to sell it. The next day his saw-mill was burned to the ground. Coretta, too, had strong views about the Negro's social standing.

But, despite this social background, Coretta had been a good student at school, with a special talent for music. She had won a scholarship to study music at Antioch College in Ohio. In 1951, when she graduated from the college, she had entered the New England Conservatory of Music in Boston to prepare for her intended career as a concert singer.

Coretta and Martin Luther King met when a mutual friend, Mary Powell, arranged a blind date for them. King made up his mind about Coretta at once. "You can talk about other things than music . . . about ideas," he told her. Driving home from that first date, he surprised her by saying, "You have all of the qualities that I expect to find in the girl I'd like to have for a wife."

But Coretta was not so sure. She knew that marrying King and becoming a minister's wife meant giving up her own career. She thought about it all through the spring and summer of 1952. Finally, in the autumn of that year, she decided that her own career must come second.

They were married by Martin Luther King, Sr., at Coretta's parents' home on 18th June, 1953. After their honeymoon they went back to Boston where Mrs. King

"Miss Scott was also impressed with King. She thought him a gentleman and not at all the bore she believed most intellectuals were. But she was not sure she wanted to marry a minister. Being a minister's wife did not fit in with the future she had planned for herself as a glamorous soprano rushing from concert to concert . . ." *Robert M. Bleiweiss, Marching to Freedom.*

continued her studies at the Conservatory and her husband worked on his doctoral thesis.

King now began to consider offers of parishes for the following year. He received many offers from churches in both the North and the South. The Kings had to decide which to accept. They both felt that it would be pleasant to stay in the North, where there was a richer cultural environment and freer atmosphere, but King felt it was his responsibility to go back to the South to help his people. Eventually, he accepted the pastorship of the Dexter Avenue Baptist Church in Montgomery, Alabama. In June, 1954, Mrs. King finished her studies at the Conservatory and the Kings moved to Alabama.

Martin Luther King and his wife, Coretta.

# 6. Dexter Avenue

The first fifteen months of the Kings' life in Montgomery were the calmest and happiest they were ever to know. King was involved in his pastoral duties and finishing his doctoral thesis. Mrs. King was expecting their first child. They had many friends, they were happy.

In the spring, King finished his thesis and began to think of his future. Should he preach and write for a few years, and then move on to an academic position, possibly at Morehouse College? This could well have happened, had events not thrust him to the head of a new movement, a new Negro revolution.

In November, 1955, the Kings' first child was born, a girl whom they named Yolanda. Three weeks later, on 1st December, a Negro seamstress named Rosa Parks, tired from working all day and shopping, refused to give up her seat on the bus to a white passenger. She later said that she had not planned to do what she did: "I was just plain tired, and my feet hurt." The bus driver called a policeman, who arrested Mrs. Parks. She was taken to the courthouse. There she was allowed to phone a man named E. D. Nixon, who was to come down and sign bail for her. E. D. Nixon, a Civil Rights activist in Montgomery, had seen his people pushed around for years. He was tired of it, he had had enough.

Suddenly it seemed as if all Negroes in Montgomery felt that way too. A one-day boycott of the buses was

*Opposite* **Martin Luther King with his daughter, Yolanda.**

planned to protest at the treatment of Negroes on the buses in Montgomery and throughout the whole state of Alabama. E. D. Nixon rang Dr. King and said, "We have taken this type of thing too long. I feel the time has come to boycott the buses. It's the only way to make the white folks see that we will not take this sort of thing any longer."

On the day of the boycott, the Kings were up at dawn. Dr. King was in the kitchen when the first bus came along the road. "Martin! Martin! come quickly!" called his wife. He ran to look: the bus was completely empty. So was the bus after that, and the one after that. Dr. King jumped into his car and drove around the city, looking at empty bus after empty bus. He felt that a miracle had happened. Negroes were walking, riding mules, driving wagons – anything to stay off the buses.

That same Monday morning Rosa Parks was convicted and fined ten dollars. Dr. King and the other Negro leaders held a meeting in the afternoon. They decided to extend the boycott until the bus company met certain minimal demands. They founded the Montgomery Improvement Association (M.I.A.) and Dr. King was asked to be the President.

The position of President was a dangerous one. It meant being singled out as the key leader of the boycott and the target for white people's anger. Dr. King accepted readily and courageously. At the meeting it was suggested that the Association should be kept secret. If no names were mentioned it would not be too dangerous for the leaders. E. D. Nixon did not like that idea: "We're acting like little boys," he said. "Somebody's name will be known, and if we're afraid we might just as well fold up right now. The white folks are going to find out anyway. We'd better decide now if we are going to be fearless men or scared little boys."

Dr. King, as President of the Montgomery Improve-

"The system that has banished personality and scarred the soul of the Negro has also damaged the white man's personality, giving him a false sense of superiority as it gives the Negro a false sense of inferiority Segregation is as bad for one as for the other." *Dr. Martin Luther King, Jr.*

ment Association, was asked to make the main speech at the mass meeting that night. He was nervous about the responsibility. He had to make a speech militant enough to inspire his people to action, and yet it was not in him to arouse hate or resentment.

He arrived at the meeting that night to find that five thousand people had gathered. After the cheers which greeted his arrival had died down, he spoke: " . . . there comes a time," he said, "when people get tired. We are here this evening to say to those who have mistreated us so long, that we are tired. Tired of being segregated and humiliated, tired of being kicked about by the brutal feet of oppression. We have no alternative but to protest . . . we have been amazingly patient. But we come here tonight to be saved from the patience that makes us patient with anything less than freedom and justice."

He talked about the comparisons the newspapers were making between the Montgomery Improvement Association and the Ku Klux Klan, "They are protesting for the perpetuation of injustice. We're protesting for the birth of justice . . . their methods lead to violence and lawlessness, but in our protest there will be no cross burnings, no white person will be taken from his home by a hooded Negro mob and brutally murdered . . . we will be guided by the highest principles of law and order . . . If you will protest courageously and yet with dignity and Christian love, future historians will say: 'There lived a great people – a black people – who injected new meaning and dignity into the veins of civilization.' This is our challenge and our overwhelming responsibility."

When he had finished speaking, the crowd rose cheering. In that speech, Dr. King had set the tempo and tenor of the movement he was to lead.

"A decisive fact confronted the Negro and helped bring him out of the houses, into the streets, out of the trenches and into the front lines. This was his recognition that one hundred years had passed since emancipation, with no profound effect on his plight." *Dr. Martin Luther King, Jr. Why We Can't Wait.*

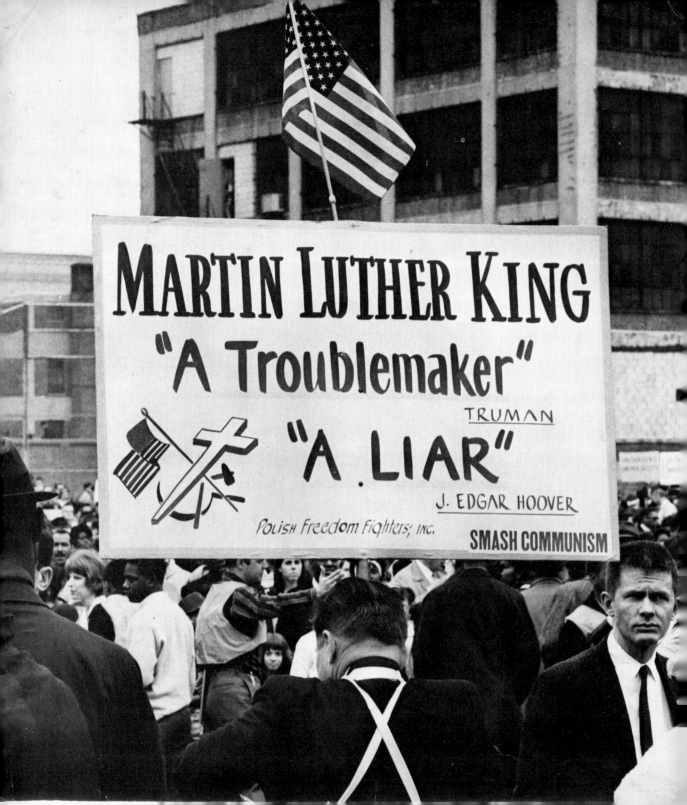

# 7. The Boycott

Dr. King realized that if the boycott was to last arrangements would have to be made to help people get to work. The Montgomery Improvement Association organized a car pool of nearly three hundred cars to drive people who needed transport. The pool was partly financed with money that poured in from supporters all over the world. In spite of this, however, thousands still had to walk. But they did it gladly. A reporter asked one old lady walking to work whether she was tired: "No," she said, "It used to be my soul was tired and my feets rested. Now my feets are tired, but my soul is rested."

Something new was happening in Montgomery. The spirit and unity of the Negro community was stronger than it had ever been. Dr. King had succeeded in the task of bringing together its different sections because he was respected by both Negro intellectuals and working people alike. They were all willing to work together in a common cause.

But it was not done easily. As the key figure in the press coverage of the boycott, Dr. King received obscene and threatening telephone calls almost daily. He was also the target for official anger. One evening as he was leaving a car park with three passengers a policeman stopped him and asked to see his licence. "It's that damn King fellow," the policeman said to his colleague. But he let Dr. King drive on until he had dropped off his

"If our white brothers are to master fear, they must depend not only on their commitment to Christian love, but also on the Christlike love which the Negro generates towards them . . . The Negro must convince the white man that he seeks justice for both himself and the white man." *Dr. Martin Luther King, Jr.*

*Opposite* **Dr. King, as President of the Montgomery Improvement Association, was the main object of the white peoples fury and there were heated demonstrations against him and the Negro Civil Rights movement.**

passengers, then he pulled alongside and arrested him for going 30 m.p.h. in a 25 m.p.h. zone. Dr. King was taken to the city jail and thrown into a cell. News of his arrest spread quickly, and people started to gather at the jail. The situation looked so bad to the police that they decided to release the "offender."

One night shortly after that, just after Dr. King had gone to bed, the telephone rang. "Listen, nigger, we've taken all we want from you; before next week you'll be sorry you ever came to Montgomery."

Three evenings later the bombing occurred. Mrs. King was chatting with a friend in the living room when there was a thud on the front porch – she later said it sounded like a brick. But the "brick" went off, shattering the porch and the front windows and filling the house with smoke. Mrs. King, unhurt but terrified, ran to where the baby was asleep at the back of the house. Luckily, Yolanda, too, had come to no harm.

By the time Dr. King, who had been at a meeting, arrived at his home, an angry crowd of Negroes had gathered outside. Police were trying to control the crowd. The situation was extremely dangerous. White reporters who had arrived at the house to cover the story were afraid to leave. The whole thing could have exploded into a disastrous race riot. Dr. King walked out onto his porch. Holding up his hands to silence the crowd he said, "My wife and baby are all right. I want you to go home and put down your weapons. We cannot solve this problem through retaliatory violence. We must meet violence with non-violence... We must meet hate with love. Remember, if I am stopped, this movement will not stop, because God is with this movement."

The people in the crowd were deeply moved by his words, many were crying. When the Police Commissioner and the Mayor told the crowd that everything possible would be done to find the people who had bombed the King's house, people began to drift away. One policeman was heard to say, "If it hadn't been for the nigger preacher we'd all be dead."

Martin Luther King (right) with another Negro leader, the Reverend R. D. Abernathy.

# 8. The First Success

The bus boycott continued. The white citizens of Montgomery were determined not to give in to the demands of the M.I.A. The demands, which were quite moderate, were as follows: courteous treatment of Negro passengers by bus drivers; seating of passengers on a first-come first-served basis, with Negroes sitting from the back of the bus to the front, and whites from front of the bus to the back; Negro drivers to work on the mainly Negro routes.

Jack Crenshaw, the attorney for the bus company, summed up the white public's attitude when he said, "If we granted these Negroes these demands, they would go about boasting they had won a victory over the white people, and this we will not stand for."

In February, 1956, a Montgomery attorney found an old state law forbidding boycotts. On the strength of it the Montgomery Grand Jury brought indictments against ninety people, including Dr. King. He was the first defendant in the trial that followed. He was found guilty, and fined five hundred dollars. His lawyers appealed against the verdict, and began proceedings in the Federal District Court against segregation on the buses.

The summer ended and still the boycott went on. But the Negroes were growing tired and unhappy about the idea of another winter of walking to work through the

*Opposite* **Martin Luther King giving a press conference when he was on trial on charges arising from the Negro bus boycott. His wife stands beside him.**

41

> "Non-violence is a powerful and just weapon. It is a weapon unique in history which cuts without wounding and ennobles the man who wields it. It is a sword that heals." *Martin Luther King, Jr., Why we Can't Wait.*

rain and snow. And white resistance had become stronger; Negroes were being beaten up, and petrol stations supplying fuel for the car pool were bombed. As if this were not enough, the police harassed Negroes at every opportunity.

On 30th October, 1956, the Mayor of Montgomery ordered legal proceedings against the car pool. Dr. King and other prominent Negroes were called to a court hearing on 13th November. In court, Montgomery attorneys said that the city had lost $15,000 in taxes because of the boycott. They asked for compensation, and an injunction against the car pool as a "public nuisance and a private enterprise operating without a licence." If this injunction was granted, and it was almost certain that it would be, it would be the end of the boycott, and the end of Dr. King's Civil Rights campaign in Montgomery.

Then, at noon on the day of the trial, a newsman handed Dr. King a note. It read: "The United States Supreme Court today affirmed a decision of a special three-judge United States District Court declaring Alabama's state and local laws requiring segregation on the buses unconstitutional." Dr. King had won his first victory – now Montgomery would have to desegregate the buses. The judge granted the injunction against the car pool, but it did not really matter. As one old man said, "God Almighty has spoken from Washington D.C."

That night Dr. King called a mass meeting to announce that the M.I.A. was ending the protest. It would take about a month for the Supreme Court order to reach Montgomery officially, and he asked everyone to delay going back to the buses until then. During that time, however, preparation for desegregation of the buses got under way. The M.I.A. printed leaflets telling people how to behave. They were asked to act courteously, no matter what insults they received. They were asked not to sit next to whites unless there were no other seats available. And, most importantly, they were not to act boastfully. As Dr. King said, "This is not a victory for Negroes alone, but for all Montgomery and for the South."

The white militant segregationists in Montgomery did everything they could to harass Negroes at this time. "Blood will run in the streets" they threatened, if desegregation was enforced.

The court order reached Montgomery on 20th December. On the morning of the following day, Dr. King was up early – again for the 6 a.m. bus. But this time he was going to be the first passenger. The bus pulled up at the stop and Dr. King climbed aboard. The bus driver said:

"I believe you are Dr. King?"

"Yes I am."

"We are glad to have you with us this morning."

Dr. King rode on different buses all that day, so did other Negro ministers and leaders, just in case there was trouble. The first day was uneventful, but the peace was soon shattered. Some night buses were shot at. Negroes were dragged off the buses and beaten up. The house and church of Reverend Ralph Abernathy, Dr. King's friend and co-worker in the movement, were bombed. On 28th January, 1957, someone again tried to bomb the King's house. Finally, the city authorities stepped in, and urged peaceful acceptance of desegregation. White businessmen announced that they were opposed to the bombings, and at last the violence ended.

> "On December 21, 1956, Dr. King got on the South Jackson Street bus. He took a seat next to the window. Rev. Glenn Smiley, a white minister from New York, got on and sat down next to Dr. King. White man and black man, side by side in Montgomery, Alabama, went for a ride on the bus." *Robert M. Bleiweiss, Marching to Freedom.*

# 9. The S.C.L.C.

The idea of non-violent protest was not new to American Negro revolutionaries. It had been recognized for a long time as the only practical means of protest for the Negro, in a country where he represents only twelve per cent of the total population. Towards the end of the Montgomery boycott, Dr. King decided that non-violence was more than just a practical method for revolution. He believed that if men would "Stand up for righteousness, stand up for truth, God would be at their side." Combining his Christian ideals with Gandhian techniques, he created a working means to express the demands of America's Negroes.

In 1956, Dr. King added a new element to the movement. Believing, like Mahatma Gandhi, that it was important to disobey unjust laws, he said, "Every man has a right and personal responsibility to break, ignore, and resist certain local laws, no matter what the personal consequences are, in order to abide by the national law." Now, on 3rd September, he had a chance to do just that. On that day he and Mrs. King were at the Montgomery courthouse. They were standing in a corridor when a policeman came up to them and told them to "move along." Dr. King explained that he was just waiting for his lawyer, Fred Gray. The policeman's only reply was, "If you don't get the hell out of here, you're going to need a lawyer." Dr. King stood firmly

> "At no other time in American history have so many people gone peaceably onto the streets to espouse a cause – in defiance often of local laws and in defiance also of the Puritan notion that going to jail is somehow a disgrace. For a great many Negroes, obviously, going to jail is no longer a shameful blot on their record; it has become a badge of honour."
> *William Brink and Louis Harris. The Negro Revolution in America.*

*Opposite* **During the bus boycott Dr. King was arrested on a driving offence and thrown into jail.**

45

The police had no sympathy for Dr. King and arrested him for very minor offences.

where he was. "Boy, you done it now," said the policeman, and, with another officer to help him, grabbed Dr. King, twisted his arms behind his back, and pushed him towards police headquarters.

When the police found out that he was Martin Luther King he was released, but he would be tried in court for disobeying an officer. Dr. King decided that if he was convicted he would go to jail: "If I commit a crime in the name of Civil Rights, I will go to jail and serve time."

He was tried, found guilty, and sentenced to be fined ten dollars with the alternative of fourteen days in jail. In a statement to the judge he said that he could not "in all good conscience" pay a fine for an act that he did not commit, and that he would willingly accept the alternative jail sentence. He had made this decision because of his "deep concern for the injustices and indignities" that his people still suffered, and because of his "love for America and the principles of liberty and equality upon which she is founded."

"The time has come," he continued, "when perhaps only the willing and non-violent acts of suffering can arouse this nation to wipe out the scourge of brutality and violence inflicted on Negroes."

By his action Dr. King showed his people that he was not afraid to go to prison, that it was even good to do so in the name of Civil Rights. He thus destroyed the power of one of the white Southerners' main instruments of fear – the jail.

In the end Dr. King did not serve the sentence. His fine was paid by the police chief, who realized there would be a great public outcry if the now famous Dr. King was imprisoned. But, just to save face, he issued a statement saying that he had paid the fine to save the taxpayer the expense of feeding Dr. King for fourteen days.

Meanwhile, several groups of Civil Rights protestors, their movements modelled on the Montgomery boycott, were making their presence felt in the South. Dr. King thought that all these efforts would be more effective if they were co-ordinated. So, on 15th February, 1957, the Southern Christian Leadership Conference (S.C.L.C.) was formed. Its purpose was to fight all forms of segregation, and to work to increase black voter registration in the South. Dr. King was made its President, and offices were opened in Atlanta, Georgia. Most of the delegates to the Conference were ministers.

One of the S.C.L.C.'s first acts was to send a telegram to the President of the United States, Dwight D. Eisenhower, urging him to hold a White House Conference on Civil Rights. The S.C.L.C. needed Federal Government support to accomplish its goals. But there was no response to the telegram. It seemed that the Federal Government was not interested. The time had come for stronger measures.

So, on 17th May, 1957, some thirty-seven thousand people gathered at the Lincoln Memorial in Washington D.C. to support the Negro Civil Rights Movement. In a speech to the demonstrators Dr. King emphasized the need for strong support from the Federal Government and from moderates in the South, and for courage from the black community.

This demonstration, the Pilgrimage of Freedom, together with increased activities of the S.C.L.C., finally persuaded President Eisenhower to hold a meeting about the Civil Rights question at the White House. At this meeting Dr. King asked the President to push through a Civil Rights bill to protect Negroes' voting rights, and to halt the bombing of Negro homes and churches. The President listened politely, but would not promise any action; "Reverend," he said, "there are so many problems–Lebanon, Algeria . . ."

"Our organization [the S.C.L.C.] was, from the first, church-oriented, both in its leadership and membership and in the ideal of non-violence – a spiritual concept in deep accord with the American Negro's Christian beliefs." *Coretta Scott King. My Life with Martin Luther King, Jr.*

# 10. National Prominence

Martin Luther King was only twenty-seven years old when the Montgomery boycott ended. He had already achieved a position of national prominence and was in great demand as a speaker. *Time* magazine called him "the scholarly Negro Baptist who in little more than a year has risen from nowhere to become one of the nation's remarkable leaders of men. His leadership extends beyond a single battle because of his spiritual force." By 1957 most major American publications had run sympathetic articles about him, as had many papers and magazines abroad. *Jet* magazine said Dr. King had become "a symbol of divinely inspired hope . . . a kind of modern Moses who has brought new self-respect to Southern Negroes."

In 1957 Dr. King delivered 208 speeches and journeyed 780,000 miles spreading the message of non-violent revolution. He received many honours: the N.A.A.C.P.'s Spingarn Medal, as the person making the greatest contribution in the field of race relations; Morehouse College gave him an honorary degree, the first of many he was to receive; and he was invited to attend the independence day celebrations of the new nation of Ghana.

In September, 1958, Dr. King's first book, *Stride Towards Freedom,* was published and received warm reviews. Dr. King agreed to make public appearances

*Opposite* **After the Montgomery boycott, Dr. King delivered many speeches calling for non-violent revolution. Here he can be seen speaking in Atlanta, Georgia.**

to help publicize the book, which is an account of the Montgomery boycott. On 19th September, he was autographing copies of his book at a department store in Harlem, the Negro section of New York City. He was seated at a desk when a heavy-set Negro woman pushed through the crowd and approached him. "Are you Dr. King?" she asked. "Yes, I am," he answered. The woman then pulled a letter opener from the front of her dress and stabbed it into Dr. King's chest. "Luther King, I have been after you for five years."

Dr. King was rushed to Harlem Hospital. It took a team of surgeons three hours to remove the letter opener. One of the doctors who performed the operation said later that the tip of the letter opener had nearly penetrated the main artery from the heart – "He was just a sneeze away from death. Had he sneezed or coughed the weapon would have penetrated the aorta."

The woman who had stabbed him, Izola Curry, was committed to the Mattewan State Hospital for the criminally insane. Dr. King's attitude towards her was one of sympathy; he hoped "all thoughtful people will do all in their power to see that she gets the help she

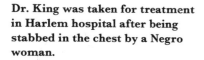

**Dr. King was taken for treatment in Harlem hospital after being stabbed in the chest by a Negro woman.**

apparently needs if she is to become a free and constructive member of society." To him the stabbing demonstrated that a climate of hatred and bitterness so permeated areas of America that deeds of extreme violence were inevitable: "Today it was I. Tomorrow it could be another leader or any man."

Dr. King was ordered by his doctors to rest after the stabbing. He decided to visit India, something he had wanted to do for a very long time, because of his admiration for Gandhi. He and his wife arrived in New Delhi on 10th February. "To other countries I may go as a tourist, but to India I come as a pilgrim," Dr. King said on his arrival. After journeying all over India, making speeches and meeting Indian leaders, he came home to America more than ever convinced that the only way to force the Government to remedy social injustice was by non-violent revolution and personal suffering.

Dr. King returned to America in 1959 to a very tense situation in the South. White militants were openly defying the Civil Rights Commission; there were bombings of Negro homes, and even lynchings.

Dr. King thought the time had come for more organized protests. He decided to resign from the pastorship of the Dexter Avenue Baptist church in order to spend more time working with the S.C.L.C. This news he announced to his parishioners on 29th November, 1959. He said that for too long he had been trying to do too much: "I can't stop now. History has thrust something upon me which I cannot turn away. I should free you now. I would like to submit my resignation as pastor of the Dexter Avenue Baptist Church . . ."

His resignation was reluctantly accepted, and as the congregation linked hands and sang "Blest be the tie that binds" Dr. King broke down and cried.

"He [Dr. King] articulates the longings, the hopes, the aspirations of his people in a most earnest and profound manner. He is a humble man, down to earth, honest. He has proved his commitment to Judeo-Christian ideals. He seeks to save the nation and its soul, not just the Negro." *Ralph Abernathy.*

# 11. The Student Movement

In 1960 a campaign to desegregate lunch counters was begun in Greensboro, North Carolina, by a black student who had read about the work of Martin Luther King. Once the story was picked up by the press, black students all over the South decided to conduct "sit-ins" to draw attention to the humiliation of being refused a meal just because of the colour of one's skin. Many carried signs saying "Remember the teachings of Gandhi and Martin Luther King."

The S.C.L.C. sponsored a meeting to help the students, and an organization was formed called the Student Non-violent Coordinating Committee (S.N.C.C., or Snick). It was during the student demonstrations that the famous rallying song of the whole Civil Rights movement was first sung. *We Shall Overcome* was a hymn originally sung by textile workers; people now sang it at rallys, sit-ins, marches, demonstrations, and in jail. It became the anthem of the movement.

Dr. King, who had now moved to Atlanta to be near the S.C.L.C. offices, worked very closely with the students. He was with a large group of them staging a sit-in at Rich's department store in Atlanta when the police arrested him with the entire group. It had been agreed beforehand that if they were arrested they would, if need be, go to jail. Dr. King said, "I'll stay

*Opposite* **In 1960, students began a campaign to desegregate lunch counters. Here they can be seen conducting a "sit-in" in a downtown Oklahoma City restaurant.**

53

**The owners of the eating places asked the demonstrators to leave, but the requests were met with silent stares and many Negroes were arrested.**

in jail one year or ten years if it takes that long to desegregate Rich's."

After several days the students were released, but Dr. King was detained. This was because the sheriff of nearby DeKalb county had asked for his custody on the grounds that he had violated his parole. Several months before, Dr. King had been arrested in DeKalb county for driving in Georgia with an Alabama licence. He had been fined twenty-five dollars and released on parole. Now the DeKalb county authorities were determined to crush "that troublemaker King."

Dr. King was brought to trial, found guilty, and sentenced to six months' imprisonment at the state penitentiary. It was a harsh sentence; his people worried about him as nobody could tell how he would be treated in this notoriously bad racial prison.

Although Mrs. King was pregnant at the time, she was determined to go to the penitentiary, a journey of three hundred miles, to take her husband the things he might need. As she was preparing to leave she received a telephone call from Senator John Kennedy, who said, "I want to express my concern about your husband. I know this must be very hard for you. I understand you are expecting a baby, and I just wanted you to know that I was thinking about you and Dr. King. If there is anything I can do to help, please feel free to call on me."

John Kennedy's brother, Robert Kennedy, then called the judge who had sentenced Dr. King to ask why the prisoner could not be released on bail. After the call it seemed that he could be. Dr. King was allowed to go home.

The story received full publicity. A few days later John Kennedy was elected President of the United States by a very small majority. It is said that his telephone call to Dr. King swung the election for him because it won him the Negro vote.

The sit-ins continued with fair success. Hundreds of lunch counters throughout the South were desegregated. Then the students came up with a new kind of protest: the "freedom ride." A committee was formed to organize freedom rides and the students asked Dr. King to be chairman of this committee. The purpose of these rides was to desegregate transportation facilities in the South. Groups of young people, both black and white, would board inter-state buses heading for the Southern states and refuse to observe the segregation laws applied to the facilities along the way.

The freedom rides made Southern reactionaries furious. They hauled riders off buses and beat them up. But the rides went on throughout the whole summer of 1961. In spite of the punishment and abuse they received, the students displayed courage and determination in continuing to demonstrate in this way.

"This generation is engaged in a cold war, not only with the earlier generation, but with the values of society. It is not the families and normal hostility of the young groping for independence. It has a new quality of bitter antagonism and confused anger which suggests basic issues are being contested."
*Dr. Martin Luther King. The Trumpet of Conscience.*

# 12. Birmingham

After Montgomery, Dr. Martin Luther King's next major campaign took place in Albany, Georgia, really hard-core racialist territory. Albany was totally segregated and life there for Negroes was miserable in the extreme. The movement in Albany began when a group of freedom riders was arrested there on 10th December, 1961. After the arrests a Negro doctor called William Anderson called Dr. King and asked for help from the S.C.L.C. Dr. King and Ralph Abernathy went to Albany, where they headed a march to City Hall to petition for integration. Although all the marchers were arrested, in the negotiations that followed the city authorities agreed to desegregate the bus and rail stations.

The movement continued with sit-ins and boycotts of stores throughout the summer. But the city authorities were unwilling to do any more. They closed the parks and public libraries rather than integrate them. In protest, Dr. King began to plan a massive demonstration, but the city officials obtained a Federal injunction against the march and Dr. King decided to call it off. He later regretted this: "Now that they're successful in getting a Federal injunction they're going to do it over and over again; and that means we will be stymied." It was the end of organized protest in Albany.

Although the Albany movement was not the same

*Opposite* **Many arrests were made during the massive protest marches in Birmingham, Alabama.**

dramatic success as the movement in Montgomery, it was useful in that the S.C.L.C. staff learned valuable lessons in community protest that were to be helpful in the next campaign – in Birmingham, Alabama.

Birmingham is a manufacturing city, one of the richest in the South. It was absolutely committed to segregation. The Mayor, Arthur Hanes, was a segregationist, and the Commissioner of Public Safety, "Bull" Connor, was an extreme racialist with a reputation for brutality. George Wallace had been elected Governor of Alabama in November, 1962, on a platform of "segregation forever."

Between 1957 and 1962 there had been seventeen bombings of Negro homes and churches. White racialists had attacked and sometimes even killed Negroes – without punishment. Dr. King said of it, "It is the most thoroughly segregated city in America. All the evils and injustices the Negro can be subjected to are right there in Birmingham."

In May, 1962, the Reverend Fred Shuttlesworth of Birmingham asked the S.C.L.C. to organize a massive anti-segregation campaign there. Dr. King thought that, "the campaign in Birmingham would surely be the toughest fight of our Civil Rights career; it could, if successful, break the back of segregation all over the nation."

The protest was to start on 12th March, 1963, after the elections for Mayor were over. Bull Connor was opposing two moderate candidates for the position and Dr. King did not want to do anything that might help Connor in this election.

The committee for the Birmingham movement laid highly organized plans for demonstration. As the movement in Albany had failed largely due to lack of organization, the protesters were determined that this should not happen in Birmingham. They decided to concentrate on various specific objectives – the desegregation of lunch counters and rest rooms, and more jobs for Negroes in the big department stores. Workshops on non-violent protest were set up by the committee throughout the Negro community, and people were recruited to help in the demonstrations. Dr. King made several trips to Birmingham to check on the organization of the movement. Money was raised all over the country to cover the costs of paying bail and legal expenses.

In January, 1963, Dr. King, along with Ralph Abernathy and Fred Shuttlesworth, met President Kennedy and the Attorney General, Robert Kennedy. Dr. King tried to persuade the Kennedys to push for Civil Rights legislation in 1963. The two Kennedys were quite sympathetic, but said they did not plan to propose any Civil Rights legislation that year.

Despite his disappointment at this, Dr. King kept his hopes high. He felt that a big confrontation like the one planned for Birmingham would force the Federal Government to act. He told the President his plans, feeling it advisable to warn him in advance. If violence flared up, the demonstrators might need Government help.

The Birmingham movement began on 3rd April, 1963. In the first three days thirty-five people were arrested at lunch counter sit-ins. Forty-five more were arrested on 6th April for parading. They all rode to jail singing freedom songs while thousands cheered from the pavements. Demonstrations were held every day, and soon there were about three hundred people in jail.

Meanwhile, Dr. King was trying to negotiate official agreement to various demands – the desegregation of store facilities, hiring of Negroes, the dropping of charges against protesters, and the creation of a

"Non-violence has passed the test of its steel in the fires of turmoil. The united power of the southern segregation was the hammer. Birmingham was the anvil." *Martin Luther King, Jr. Why we Can't Wait.*

bi-racial committee to work for further desegregation in Birmingham. The business community was willing to talk, but the city government was not.

The city officials got an injunction against the demonstrators issued by a state court, not a Federal court. Dr. King refused to obey it. He chose Good Friday, 12th April, as the day when he and other leaders would break the injunction and provoke arrest.

The march was to start from the Zion Hill Church. Dr. King spoke to his people before they moved off about the state of things in Birmingham, a situation which he thought could only be changed by suffering. Determined to risk going to jail if need be, he led the marchers slowly towards the city's downtown section. Negroes lined the streets singing *We shall overcome* as the column of demonstrators approached.

At that point Bull Connor decided he had seen enough. "Don't let them go any farther!" he shouted. Dr. King and several other demonstrators were arrested. Dr. King was held in jail completely incommunicado. He was not even allowed to call his wife, and no-one was allowed to talk to him.

By the following Sunday, Mrs. King, greatly troubled about her husband's fate, decided to ring President Kennedy. She finally reached Robert Kennedy, who promised to help her. The next day President Kennedy rang her to say that he had just talked to the Birmingham authorities, that Dr. King was safe and would be calling her soon. Fifteen minutes later Dr. King was on the 'phone to his wife. He was delighted to hear about the President's intervention, and told Mrs. King to issue a press statement.

He stayed in jail for eight days. During his imprisonment he wrote his famous "Letter from Birmingham Jail." This was addressed to a group of white ministers who had made a statement to the press saying that

"The Negro freedom movement would have been historic and worthy even if it had only served the cause of Civil Rights. But its laurels are greater because it stimulated a broader social movement that elevated the moral level of the nation."
*Martin Luther King, Jr., in a talk given in 1967.*

60

they thought the protest "unwise and untimely" and that Dr. King was a publicity-seeking outside agitator. "I am in Birmingham because injustice is here," declared Dr. King, and went on in his letter to explain the philosophy of the movement, and what the attitude of all Christians should be toward it. He denounced white moderates who were more concerned with order than justice. He said, "One day the South will know that when these disinherited children of God sat down at lunch-counters, they were in reality standing up for what is best in the American Dream and for the most sacred values of our Judeo-Christian heritage . . ."

Dr. King was released from the Birmingham jail on 20th April. That night he and the other leaders of the protest worked out a new plan for the crusade. They decided to recruit Birmingham's black school children for the demonstration. Dr. King thought it was time to give the movement "a dramatic new dimension." He felt that as it was the children who would benefit most from desegregation, taking part in the demonstration would give them a sense of value and achievement. Young people from the Birmingham high schools and colleges joined the crusade by the thousand, going to training sessions in non-violent protest.

On 2nd May they were ready. Dr. King addressed the first group of young people at the Sixteenth Street Baptist Church. Then they marched towards the downtown area, singing *We Shall Overcome*. They were all arrested. After that, more came. Group after group of young people marched downtown only to be arrested – 959 in all on that first day.

The next day Police Chief Bull Connor massed police in the street all around the Sixteenth Street Baptist Church. One thousand children left the church and began marching downtown. "We want freedom," they chanted, ignoring police orders to stop. A furious Bull

During the protest marches in Birmingham, Alabama, thousands of Negroes roamed the streets shouting slogans like "Freedom, Freedom."

61

Connor ordered high-powered fire hoses to be turned on them. Crushing jets of water battered the youngsters down as their horrified parents looked on. Then the battle began. Bottles and bricks were brought out and hurled at the police, who released their dogs among the demonstrators. "Look at 'em run," Connor said, "look at those niggers run." Two hours later it was all over. The marchers were driven back to the church – but they felt far from defeated. "We're going on in spite of dogs and fire hoses," said Dr. King. "We've gone too far to turn back."

The children went on demonstrating all the next week. Finally, so many had been arrested that the jails

**Many of the children who demonstrated in Birmingham were arrested and detained in a state fairground building until the authorities decided to release them.**

were overflowing and the police could make no more arrests. The children knew this and at one point three thousand young people marched around the police lines, up and down the streets, in and out of the department stores, singing freedom songs, safe in the knowledge that the police could do nothing to stop them. As the situation grew more tense the Governor of Alabama, George Wallace, called out the National Guard. Pressure was building up all over the nation. Television and newspaper pictures showing children being beaten and hosed aroused people, and hundreds of telegrams poured into the White House demanding that something be done. President Kennedy sent Burke Marshall, Deputy Attorney General in charge of Civil Rights, to Birmingham to try to arrange negotiations.

At first the white leaders stubbornly refused to negotiate. It looked as if nothing could be done. Then, on 7th May, as a number of white leaders broke up a meeting to go to lunch, they found the streets lined with black people. As Dr. King said, "There were square blocks of Negroes, a veritable sea of black faces. They were committing no violence, they were just present and singing. Downtown Birmingham echoed to the strains of the freedom songs." This demonstration so impressed the white leaders that they came out from lunch ready to talk terms for the first time. On 10th May an agreement was reached: stores were to be desegregated, charges against the demonstrators would be dropped, and there would be regular meetings between black leaders and the white business councils.

The victory in Birmingham was the biggest for the movement so far; it cracked the whole structure of discrimination in the South and gave Negroes a new sense of pride. As President Kennedy remarked, "Bull Connor has done as much for Civil Rights as Abraham Lincoln."

# 13. The Nobel Prize

As a result of the events in Birmingham many people all over America were won over to the cause of racial equality. Wherever Dr. King went to speak, huge crowds turned up to hear him. He was no longer speaking to his people alone, he was addressing the conscience of all America. He particularly inspired young people. His appeals for a reassessment of American morality inspired not only the Black Revolution, but also the anti-Vientnam War crusade, the Student Revolution, and even set the scene for the Women's Liberation Movement.

On 28th August, 1963, 250,000 people took part in a march on Washington and heard Dr. King make his now-famous "I have a Dream" speech.

Then, less than three weeks after the glowing success of the Washington march, tragedy struck in Birmingham. One quiet Sunday morning the calm was shattered by a tremendous explosion. In the Sixteenth Street Baptist Church, four little Negro girls lay dead and several people were injured. The bomb had exploded during Sunday School, when more than four hundred people had been in the church. "In church!" a woman screamed, "My God, you're not even safe in church!"

Horrified, Dr. King raced to Birmingham to give what comfort he could. At the funeral service for the

*Opposite* **Dr. Martin Luther King was presented with the Nobel Prize for Peace in 1964 by the President of the Nobel Prize Committee, Dr. Gunnar Jahn.**

65

The body of a young Negro girl
is put in an ambulance after a
bomb in a Baptist Church had
killed four children and injured
23 other people.

children he said: "Their death says to us that we must work passionately and unceasingly to make the American Dream a reality. They did not die in vain. The innocent blood of these little girls may well serve as the redemptive force that will bring a new light to this dark city."

Tragedy struck again that year, on a fine November morning in Dallas, Texas. President Kennedy was shot and killed by a man called Lee Harvey Oswald, whose motive was never discovered. Dr. King, filled with grief, returned to Washington for the funeral. He had lost a friend, a friend whose fate troubled him deeply. "This is what is going to happen to me also," Dr. King told his wife.

The summer of 1964 was a difficult and active one for Dr. King. He was involved in voter registrations and the movement to integrate public facilities. His life seemed to be one long round of speech-making. Mrs. King had become anxious about his health, and persuaded him to go into hospital for a check-up and a rest. While he was in hospital he learned that he had been named the winner of the Nobel Peace Prize. "I am glad that people of other nations are concerned with our problems here," was his comment. He announced that the money from the Prize would be divided among the various organizations involved in the movement. He did not consider this intended for him personally, "but a tribute to the disciplined, wise restraint and majestic courage of gallant Negro and white persons of goodwill who have followed a non-violent course in seeking to establish . . . a rule of love across this nation of ours."

Dr. and Mrs. King went with some close friends to Oslo, Norway, for the prize-giving ceremonies. In his citation Dr. Jahn, head of the Nobel Committee, said, "Dr. King has succeeded in keeping his followers to the principle of non-violence. Without Dr. King's confirmed effectiveness of this principle, demonstrations and marches could easily have been violent and ended with the spilling of blood."

In his acceptance speech, Dr. King pointed out that "this prize has been given to me for something that really has not yet been achieved. It is a commission to go out and work harder for the things in which we believe."

Dr. King was given a hero's welcome when he arrived back in New York. Fire boats on the river jetted streams of water, and Mayor Robert Wagner presented him with the key to the city. The next day the Kings had lunch with the Governor of New York.

After the festivities came to an end, Dr. King spoke to a huge rally in Harlem: "For the last several days I have been on a mountain top, and I really wish I could just stay on the mountain, but I must go back to the valley. I must go back, because my brothers and sisters down in Mississippi and Alabama are sweltering under the heat of injustice. There are people starving in the valley, and people who don't have jobs, and people who can't vote."

The Kings returned home, where the Ebenezer Baptist Church had arranged a tribute to their hero. When the city of Atlanta later held a testimonial dinner for Dr. King fifteen hundred people, black and white, attended. There were speeches and tributes, and at the end of the ceremonies everybody joined hands and sang *We Shall Overcome*. For one night, in a Southern city, hate and prejudice *had* been overcome.

"I say good night to you by quoting the words of an old Negro slave preacher, who said, 'We ain't what we ought to be and we ain't what we want to be and we ain't what we're going to be. But Thank God, we ain't what we was'." *Dr. Martin Luther King, speaking in Los Angeles, California.*

"There was a man called Alfred Nobel. He was a millionaire. And when he died he said that he would like to have a Peace Prize. The man who made the most peace – he would get $54,600. There were three Negroes to win the Peace Prize. The first was Ralph Bunche in 1950. The second was Chief Albert J. Luthuli. The third was my daddy." *Yolanda King, daughter of Martin Luther King.*

# 14. Selma, Alabama

In 1964 the Civil Rights Bill which President Kennedy had sent to Congress was passed, and signed into law by the new President, Lyndon Baines Johnson. Dr. King was invited to the White House by the President to be present at the signing.

Johnson was running for President that year against a conservative, Senator Barry Goldwater. Dr. King did not formally endorse Johnson, but he did speak against Goldwater. He felt that the Goldwater reactionary platform would greatly hinder his Civil Rights movement. His attacks helped Johnson win an enormous victory in the election.

Towards the end of 1964 the S.C.L.C. launched a campaign for voter registration in the deep South. Negroes were having great difficulty registering to vote, in spite of the Federal law guaranteeing this right. Dr. King decided to open the campaign in Selma, Alabama, immediately after New Year's day. He had been warned that he would be in real danger in Selma – there was a chance of violence from the strongly racialist white community there. The first casualty of the campaign occurred in Marion, a small town nearby. There had been several arrests there, and a small march was planned from the church to the Marion jail. They marched at night, and in the middle of the demonstration the street lights were switched off.

*Opposite* **Martin Luther King (in the white cap) and his wife, lead the march into Montgomery at the end of the 54 mile march from Selma.**

State troopers attempt to break up a march at Selma, where the demonstrators were protesting against the voter registration procedures.

Then the police and other whites charged the marchers, and a young boy was shot and killed while trying to protect his mother.

More demonstrations followed, and, in February, 1965, Dr. King was arrested for leading a march in Selma. While he was in prison, Malcolm X, one of the young leaders of the Black Muslims, arrived in town. The Black Muslims did not believe in desegregation – quite the contrary. They wanted to separate blacks and whites even further, so that blacks could have their own social structure. They promoted a concept of "Black Power," and advocated violence to overthrow the system. Malcolm X's presence in Selma, combined with Dr. King's imprisonment, aroused the Negro community. Mrs. King met Malcolm X, who assured her that he had not come to Selma to make things tougher for her husband: "I really did come thinking I could make it easier. If the white people realize what the alternative is, perhaps they will be more willing to hear Dr. King."

Dr. King in fact agreed with much of what the Black Muslims advocated. He believed in racial pride, in the idea that "black is beautiful;" he believed that the American Negro had the right to "freedom now," but he never, ever, believed in violence.

After his release from prison, Dr. King was in and out of Selma. The S.C.L.C. was having daily trouble registering voters; Negroes were being kept standing in lines for hours, and then told that the registration office was closed. Dr. King flew to Washington to talk to President Johnson about the situation in Alabama. He asked the President to propose a Voting Rights Bill which would include a provision for Federal registrars, to make sure voters could register. When he returned to Selma he decided to organize a march from there to Montgomery, the capital of Alabama, to demonstrate for such a Voting Rights Bill. Governor George Wallace issued an order prohibiting the march. Dr. King ignored it.

On Sunday, 7th March, five hundred black men and women started to march out from Selma. What happened next was seen by the nation on television. The marchers were ordered to turn around. There was a minute of silence, then, shouting "Get those goddam niggers!" the troops dispersed the unarmed demonstrators by swinging clubs, throwing tear gas, and wielding bull whips.

Undaunted, Dr. King announced that he and Ralph Abernathy would lead a new march on the following Tuesday. The nation had been appalled by what it had seen, but Governor Wallace still managed to obtain a Federal injunction against this march. Once again Dr. King had to decide whether to break a Federal law. He made a national appeal for people to join him in

"I stand before you this afternoon with the conviction that segregation in Alabama is on its death bed . . . We are on the move now, and no wave of racism can stop us. Let us march on to the realization of the American Dream." *Dr. Martin Luther King, in his speech in Montgomery after the march from Selma.*

Selma. And they did. People poured into Selma from all over the country to offer their support – so great was the response that Dr. King felt confident to go ahead.

The day came, and Dr. King led fifteen hundred people out of Selma. More than half of them were white. When they reached the ranks of the troopers, they were ordered to halt. As all fifteen hundred men and women knelt in the street to pray, Dr. King, fearing a repetition of what had happened only a few days before, decided to turn back. For this he was criticized, but he did not regret it – the danger had been too great, he said.

That evening he was planning what action to take next to help the campaign in Selma, when white extremists committed an act of such brutality that the nation could no longer ignore what was happening there. One evening a man called James Reeb, a white Unitarian minister from Boston and father of five children, had dinner in a Negro owned restaurant with two other ministers. As they left the restaurant, they were attacked by four Ku Klux Klansmen. Reeb's skull was crushed with a plank and he died two days later. People everywhere were outraged. Demonstrations were held throughout the country, including one in which four thousand people gathered in Washington to urge the passage of the Voting Rights Bill. President Johnson, speaking to the nation on television, said, "What happened in Selma is part of a far larger movement which reaches into every section and state of America. It is the effort of American Negroes to secure for themselves the full blessings of American life. Their cause must be our cause too. Because it is not just Negroes, but really all of us, who must overcome the crippling legacy of bigotry and injustices. And we shall overcome!" He gave the Voting

"Why must good men die for good? James Reeb's death may cause the white South to come to terms with its conscience."
*Dr. Martin Luther King, speaking at the Memorial service for James Reeb.*

In spite of all of this – the two murders, Johnson's speech, 3,800 arrests – there were still only fifty Negroes registered to vote in the area. Then the Federal injunction against the march from Selma to Montgomery was lifted. Governor Wallace gave orders forbidding it, but President Johnson sent Federal troops to protect the marchers. On Sunday, 21st March, Dr. King led five thousand people out of Selma. They marched about eight miles, then most dropped out by agreement with the Federal offices, and three hundred continued. On Thursday, the march reached Montgomery and three hundred marchers were joined by supporters from all over the country. Fifty thousand people finally marched into Montgomery.

The Selma campaign was eventually successful – the Voting Rights Bill was made law, and many thousands of new supporters, white as well as black, had joined the ranks of Martin Luther King's Civil Rights movement.

**Local and state police halt a protest march in Montgomery. The marchers were protesting against the treatment of Negro civil rights demonstrators in Selma.**

DEPLORES OUR RACIALLY
Schools
LOVE
AMERICAN
FOR
MARCHES
EQUAL RIGHTS
AND
EQUAL OPPORTUNITY
INTER
LADIES
MARCHE
76
BOSTO

# 15. The National Movement

The Voting Rights Bill became law in August, 1965. Combined with the 1964 Civil Rights Act, it represented a great advance in Negro Rights. Martin Luther King now felt that the movement must be expanded to include cities and areas in the North, and in the West. Two weeks after the Voting Rights Bill was signed, terrible race rioting broke out in the Watts district of Los Angeles. **Dr. King travelled to Watts immediately,** and went through the area talking to the people.

In the early days of the Civil Rights Campaign Dr. King had realized its effect would be immense, and would trigger off demands for desegregation from all over the country. He felt that it was his duty to be involved in this. He knew that he was most effective as a persuader, someone who could come into a tense situation and convince people that more would be accomplished if non-violent means were used. In riots it was usually the poor people, the blacks, who got hurt. It was their property that was destroyed, their people who were injured. Riots also allowed white people to salve their consciences by saying that if Negroes behaved in this way they did not deserve the rights they were demanding. This was what Dr. King had to prevent.

He and the members of the S.C.L.C. discussed which city to use as a base for the campaign in the North.

*Opposite* **Martin Luther King surrounded by demonstrators as he leads a civil rights march in Boston.**

They decided on Chicago, and a project was set up by the S.C.L.C. to focus attention on the plight of people living in urban ghettos.

While Negroes living in the North did not have to face legal discrimination, they still had to live with it as a fact of life. Because they were poor they could only afford to live in the worst city slums. Here they existed in an atmosphere of depression, sadness and lethargy. Local schools were inadequate, health facilities poor and police protection scanty. Why try to work hard to send your children to school, Negroes asked, when the school was so bad? Why work to buy nice things for your home only to get them stolen by a poorer black brother? Why work at all when the jobs available pay little more than the social security payments for the unemployed? How is it possible to improve your situation, living under such circumstances?

In January, 1966, the S.C.L.C. opened an office in Chicago, and Dr. King moved to the city with his wife and four children. He felt that he and his words would do more if he actually lived in a ghetto himself. They lived in a small slum flat until the end of the summer, while Dr. King organized the movement in Chicago. It was a new and revealing experience for the Kings to live with the poverty and hopelessness of ghetto life. His presence in the ghetto had a great effect on the morale of local people. They would come to him to talk about their problems – so many that it hardly seemed worth just trying to tackle one or two. They had almost given up, these poor slum people. Dr. King needed all his patience, energy and determination to show them what they could do to improve their situation. He encouraged them to hold back rent payments until landlords had repaired plumbing and heating. He urged people to keep their houses and streets looking clean and tidy. He understood only too

*Opposite* **This time it was just a joke, but real violence was well known in the littered streets of Harlem, the Negro area of New York.**

76

Race riots frequently broke out in the Negro ghetto area of the large towns, and the police used violent methods to break them up.

well that all these little things did not really get to the heart of the problem – but it was a beginning.

At first the young blacks resented having Dr. King in the area. They thought of him as an outside official who neither cared about them nor understood their situation. One day a teenage gang went to the King's flat, where Mrs. King and some of the S.C.L.C. members were sitting talking. The gang had come to protest about the white members of the S.C.L.C. staff – they were not wanted in the area. Mrs. King tried to explain that many white people were involved in the cause, and that some had even died in Civil Rights demonstrations. The atmosphere was growing quite tense when Dr. King, who had been sleeping, came into the room. Surprised, the youngsters asked, "Is that really you? Is that really Martin Luther King?"

"This is me. I'm Martin Luther King."

"You don't mean to tell me I'm sitting here with this cat who's been up there talking to Presidents! He's been up there eating fillet mignon steaks, and now he's sitting here eating barbeque just like me!"

Dr. King's presence in the ghetto was of paramount importance to the Chicago campaign. As he worked more and more with teenage gangs, they grew very protective towards him. They told him not to worry about having guards or police for protection – they would take care of him.

One of Dr. King's major aims in Chicago was to soften the attitude of these youngsters towards violence. He held workshops on non-violence, trying to show them how to use their energies constructively. Eventually many gang members did join the non-violent movement, and demonstrated with Dr. King. It was no mean achievement.

On 10th July, 1966, a rally and demonstration took place that the S.C.L.C. had been organizing since October, 1965. It was held at Soldiers Field in Chicago and fifty thousand people turned out for it. After the speeches Dr. King read out a list of demands that were part of a detailed plan to bring about racial justice in Chicago. He led the demonstrators on a march from Soldiers Field to City Hall to present these demands to the Mayor of Chicago.

The next day Dr. King met Mayor Daley to discuss these demands. The Mayor rejected them out of hand. Word of this spread rapidly throughout the city, and that night violence erupted. During the two nights of rioting that followed, Dr. King spent all the time in the street, trying to calm the rioters and stop the violence.

Dr. King continued to lead demonstrations in Chicago; their main target was open housing. Finally an agreement was reached on this issue between the city officials and Dr. King, but the officials did not really keep their part of the agreement – perhaps they had never intended to. Dr. King was sure that if the agreement had been implemented there would have been less racial trouble in the North.

"A lot of people are re-examining their motives. Even if this means that a lot of hidden prejudices have been uncovered in Northerners, good will be gained from the fact that Americans have been forced to act on days other than on Brotherhood days and weeks." *Arthur Brazier, a Baptist Minister.*

# 16. The Last Campaign

Early in 1967 Dr. King took up a cause which had nothing to do with race – he began to speak out against America's involvement in the Vietnam war. He was greatly criticized for taking this stand, as certain people felt he was wrong to divert his energies in this direction. To Dr. King, however, it was a moral necessity: "I know I'm right. I know this is an unjust and evil war. I have made my decision to oppose it, and whatever people say I am going to stick to my conviction."

Many more race riots hit America in the summer of 1967. Some people, especially Negroes, were saying that the non-violent movement had failed. Everywhere Dr. King spoke that summer he was hounded by the press with questions about the riots. He would answer, "I condemn the violence of the riots; but I understand the conditions that cause them. I think we must be just as concerned about correcting those conditions as we are about punishing the guilty." But would America face up to what were basically moral issues? Dr. King had his doubts: "I seriously question the will and moral power of this nation to save itself."

Towards the end of the summer Dr. King decided that the only solution to these problems was to improve jobs and economic opportunities for all poor people. He began talking about a campaign that would take poor people to Washington to plead their cause before

*Opposite* **Dr. Martin Luther King addresses anti-Vietnam war demonstrators at a protest rally in New York.**

the various Government agencies. But it would be a demonstration of poor people of all races.

The plan was approved by the board of the S.C.L.C., and work began on organizing it. Dr. King wanted to involve as many people as he could in this campaign, to show them the alternative way to air their grievances and frustrations – the peaceful way. He began touring the country to recruit people for the march. In March, 1968, he held a successful meeting with leaders of various minority groups, such as Indians, Mexican Americans and Puerto Ricans. Although the specific problems of the groups differed, they all had one thing in common – poverty.

Mrs. King has said of this period, when her husband was organizing the Poor People's Campaign: "Beyond everything there was a sense of fate closing in." Years earlier Dr. King had said that he knew he would not lead a long life. Friends remember that he talked often of the risk of being killed because of the work he did. He knew that many men who had taken a strong moral stand had paid for their convictions with their lives. He would talk about this in his speeches: "I may be crucified for my beliefs, and if I am you can say, 'He died to make men free.' "

But he never allowed such thoughts to depress him. He knew that if he did it would immobilize him, and he would be unable to do anything: "I cannot worry about my safety; I cannot live in fear. I have to function. If there is one fear I have conquered it is the fear of death."

During the planning of the Poor People's Campaign Dr. King worked harder than usual to make sure his staff was prepared to carry on without him. More than once at board meetings he told them, "If anything happens to me, you must be prepared to continue." While the Poor People's Campaign was gathering pace,

"The quality, not the longevity, of one's life is what is important. If you are cut down in a movement that is designed to save the soul of a nation then no other death could be more redemptive." *Dr. Martin Luther King.*

some trouble occurred in Memphis, Tennessee. There the garbage collectors, most of whom were black, had gone on strike because they were being unfairly treated. On 23rd February, 1968, a peaceful demonstration had been brutally broken up by police using clubs and squad cars. People were outraged, and Dr. King was asked to lead a big protest march there on 28th March. Although already overworked, he agreed to go as he would not have to do any organizing – only head the march.

But the local people who did the organizing had not done a very good job, and it was not until the march had started that Dr. King realized this. Black Power posters were being carried by some of the marchers, and, worse still, some young blacks, not marchers, but using the march as a cover, began to throw rocks.

Martin Luther King links arms with Rev. Ralph Abernathy and Rev. Ralph Jackson during the violent civil rights march in Memphis.

The police moved in. In the battle that followed many were injured, and one boy was killed. Although there was nothing Dr. King could have done to save the situation once the violence had erupted, he felt responsible for the incident. He felt discouraged, shaken, and in this mood he went back to Atlanta to ask the S.C.L.C. if they would still sponsor the protest in Memphis. He wanted a positive answer.

People had been frightened by what had happened in Memphis – rightly so. But how would this affect their attitude to the whole non-violent movement? Would they lose faith entirely? Dr. King feared so, and now his main task was to prove that the principle of **non-violent protest** *could* work – in Memphis or anywhere else.

He finally succeeded in persuading the S.C.L.C. to agree to the Memphis campaign. They sent their best organizers to arrange a march there on 8th April. Dr. King arrived on Wednesday, 3rd April. A meeting took place that night, and he spoke about the many threats against his life: "I don't know what will happen now. We've got some difficult days ahead. But it doesn't matter to me now because I've been to the mountain top, I won't mind. Like anybody else, I would like to live a long life. But I'm not concerned about that now. I just want to do God's will. And He's allowed me to go up to the mountains. And I've looked over, and I've seen the Promised Land. I may not get there with you, but I want you to know tonight that we as a people will get to the Promised Land."

The following evening just before dinner, Dr. King went out onto the balcony of his motel room, in Memphis. "Be sure to sing 'Precious Lord, Take my Hand' for me tonight, Ben, sing it real pretty," he said to Ben Branch. Solomon Jones, who was Dr. King's driver for that evening called up to him, "It's getting

"He [Dr. King] would probably say that if death had to come, I am sure there was no greater cause to die for than fighting to get a just wage for garbage collectors. He was supra race, supra denomination, supra class, and supra culture. He belonged to the world and to mankind. Now he belongs to posterity."
*Dr. Benjamin Mays, Eulogy at Dr. Martin Luther King's funeral.*

84

chilly, Dr. King, better take an overcoat." It was almost time for them to leave for dinner, when suddenly a shot rang out. The bullet hit Dr. King in the right side of the neck. He was rushed to hospital. One hour later he was dead, a victim of the violence that for so many years he had tried to prevent.

**Martin Luther King standing on the balcony of the Memphis motel the day before he was shot by an assassin.**

# Epilogue

The world mourned the death of Martin Luther King. In America, the grief found an outlet in violence. In the six days following the assassination of Dr. King by James Earl Ray, a white man, thirty four people were killed, thousands injured, and millions of dollars worth of property destroyed.

It seemed as though everything the dead man had ever stood for and worked for was now forgotten, and that those who had once marched with him would turn to those young black leaders who advocated violence.

At the time of his death, much had been gained by Dr. King's Civil Rights movement; segregation had been outlawed in the South, and it was now illegal to discriminate against Negroes in employment and housing. America's Negroes knew that non-violent protest could work, but now, leaderless and angry, what would they do?

The way they chose is perhaps the greatest tribute of all to the leadership of Martin Luther King. The violence subsided, and the movement continued – with deepened feeling. In the words of one biographer, "It is as if Dr. King's death did more to stir the conscience of his country than did his life."

Progress in obtaining social justice for Negroes has gone on steadily in the years following Dr. King's

*Opposite* **Thousands of marchers follow the funeral procession of Martin Luther King.**

assassination. Negroes have won many political victories, often in predominantly white areas. One outstanding example of this was the election in May, 1973, of a Negro – Thomas Bradley – as Mayor of Los Angeles, a city where Negroes form only 16 per cent of the population. Although there are still proportionately few elected black officials in American government, greater political advances are being made by Negroes every year.

Equally encouraging are the statistics on the type of work now available to Negroes. Between 1960 and 1970 the number of Negroes employed in technical and professional work increased by 100 per cent. The numbers of Negro schoolteachers, television announcers, lawyers, doctors and policemen working alongside their white colleagues is ever-increasing – a change indeed from the situation of ten years ago.

Better opportunities in the field of education and at work, a bigger wage packet, a greater political awareness and power – these are the hopeful signs for America's Negroes. Yet many critical problems remain to be solved. There is still a tremendous difference between the average standards of living of blacks and whites. Unemployment figures for Negroes are far greater than for whites. Many black ghettos remain, and racial violence and intolerance are still features of American life.

The "march to freedom," begun so many years ago by Martin Luther King, has achieved much; but its end is still not yet in sight.

# Principal Characters

Abernathy, Ralph (Born 1926). Black minister in Montgomery, Alabama; friend of Martin Luther King; Civil Rights leader.

Connor, Eugene "Bull" (Born 1897). Commissioner of Public Safety, Birmingham.

Dubois, W. E. B. (1868–1963). American Civil Rights leader; author.

Eisenhower, Dwight David (1890–1969). President of the United States, 1952–1960.

Johnson, Lyndon B. (1908–1973). President of the United States, 1963–1968.

Kennedy, John F. (1917–1963). President of the United States, 1960–1963.

Kennedy, Robert F. (1925–1968). Brother of John F. Kennedy; Attorney General of the United States of America.

King, Coretta Scott (Born 1927). Wife of Martin Luther King.

King, Martin Luther Sr. Father of Martin Luther King.

Malcolm X (1925–1965). Black Muslim leader; assassinated in 1965.

Nixon, E. D. Black Civil Rights activist in Alabama, co-worker of Martin Luther King.

Wallace, George (Born 1919). Governor of Alabama at the time of the Birmingham Campaign.

# Table of Dates

1961   Civil Rights Movement begins in Albany, Georgia
1963   Birmingham movement begins. Martin Luther arrested in Birmingham and later released. Children's march in Birmingham. March on Washington; "I have a dream" speech. Bombing of the Sixteenth Street Baptist Church. Assassination of President John F. Kennedy
1967   Martin Luther King receives the Nobel Peace Prize. Civil Rights Bill becomes law
1965   Selma campaign begins. March from Selma to Montgomery
1966   S.C.L.C. establishes offices in Chicago. Rally at Soldiers Field; riots in Chicago
1967   Organization of the Poor People's Campaign begins
1968   Police brutality to demonstrators in Memphis. Martin Luther King goes to Memphis. Assassination of Martin Luther King. Riots throughout America as a result of the assassination

# Glossary

BOYCOTT   Collective refusal to have any dealings with a person or institution as a means of protest.

FEDERAL   Pertaining to the central government of a union of states, distinct from the individual governments of the separate states.

INDICTMENT   A formal accusation presented by a jury, usually necessary for serious crimes.

INJUNCTION   A judicial process or order requiring the person or persons to whom it is directed to do or not to do a particular thing.

PAROLE   The liberation of a person from prison, conditional upon good behaviour, prior to the end of the maximum sentence imposed upon that person.

PLATFORM   A principle on which a party takes its stand in appealing to the public.

VOTER REGISTRATION   Placing one's name on the list of voters, which is necessary before one is allowed to vote.

WORKSHOP   Sessions organized to educate people in methods of action, such as those used in protest movements.

# Further Reading

Bennett, Lerone. *What Manner of Man* (Johnson Publishing Co. Inc., 1964). Biography of Martin Luther King, Jr. up to the year 1964. Very readable and informative.

Davis, John O. *The American Negro Reference Book* (Prentice Hall, 1966). A summary of current information on major aspects of Negro life in America. Deals with the Negro situation in the past as well as current affairs. Detailed and scholarly, for the older reader.

Drink, William and Harris, Louis. *The Negro Revolution in America* (Simon and Schuster, 1964). Based on a survey of Negro opinion made by *Newsweek* magazine in 1963, this book gives opinions of Negroes on such questions as "What is it like to be a Negro?", "Which leaders do you support?", "What are your real feelings towards whites?" Suitable for older readers.

Ezekiel, Nissim. *A Martin Luther King Reader* (Popular Prakashan, 1969). A collection of chapters from books by Martin Luther King Jr., and some of his speeches.

Franklin, John Hope. *From Slavery to Freedom* (Vintage, 1969). A classic history of the American Negro. A very scholarly study, suitable for older readers.

King, Coretta Scott. *My Life with Martin Luther King Jr.* (Hodder and Stoughton, 1969). An autobiography of the wife of Martin Luther King Jr. Very readable and informal, yet filled with much factual information about the life and works of Dr. King.

King, Martin Luther. *Strength to Love* (Harper and Row, 1958). An explanation of Dr. King's philosophies of life, religion and politics. Again, for the older reader.
*Why We Can't Wait* (Harper and Row, 1958). Written by Dr. King as an explanation of the aims of the Civil Rights Movement. Suitable for older readers.

# Index

# Picture Credits

The author and publishers wish to thank all those who have given permission for the reproduction of copyright illustrations on the following pages: United States Information Service, *jacket* (front); Camera Press, *frontispiece*; Black Star, *jacket* (back), 8, 10–11, 18, 22, 31, 32, 36, 44, 46, 48; Associated Press Photos, 39, 40, 50, 52, 54, 56, 61, 62, 66, 68, 70, 73, 74, 77, 78, 80, 83, 85, 86; Keystone, 12, 14; Radio Times Hulton Picture Library, 12, 14. All other illustrations appearing in this book are from the Wayland Picture Library.